D0481500

Yosemite Meditations

WITH PHOTOGRAPHY BY MICHAEL FRYE

FOREWORD BY
MICHAEL TOLLEFSON,
SUPERINTENDENT, YOSEMITE NATIONAL PARK

YOSEMITE ASSOCIATION, YOSEMITE NATIONAL PARK, CALIFORNIA
HEYDAY BOOKS, BERKELEY, CALIFORNIA

Design by Melanie Doherty Design, San Francisco.
Project coordination by Steven P. Medley.
All photographs by Michael Frye.

Library of Congress Cataloging-in-Publication Data
Yosemite meditations / with photography by Michael Frye ; foreword by Michael Tollefson.
    p. cm.
  Originally published: El Portal, CA : Yosemite Association, 2003.
  ISBN-13: 978-1-59714-094-2 (hardcover : alk. paper)
  1. Yosemite National Park (Calif.)--Pictorial works. 2. Quotations, English. I. Frye,
Michael, photographer.
  F868.Y6Y487 2008
  979.4'4700222--dc22
                                    2007045429

Front Cover: Cathedral Rocks reflected in the Merced River

Orders, inquiries, and correspondence should be addressed to:
        Heyday Books, P. O. Box 9145, Berkeley, CA 94709
        (510) 549-3564, Fax (510) 549-1889
        www.heydaybooks.com

Printed in Singapore

10 9 8 7 6 5 4 3 2

Within National Parks is room—

glorious room—room in which to find ourselves,

in which to think and hope,

to dream and plan, to rest and resolve.

—ENOS MILLS

FOREWORD

Yosemite is an extraordinary, wonderful place. Its towering cliffs
and domes fill us with awe, its thundering waterfalls, sinuous
rivers, and seasonal creeks inspire us, and its amazing animals
and varied plants remind us of our ties to the natural world.

This little book filled with remarkable images of the park
paired with quotes about nature and the environment provides
a delightful way to contemplate Yosemite's special qualities and
values. It is guaranteed to provoke thought about this park's
significance, the importance of all national parks and natural areas,
and the role we each play in caring for and protecting all of them.

You can read *Yosemite Meditations* alone, in moments of
solitude in a park meadow or atop a high country peak. You can
share it with others on a backpacking or camping trip. However
you choose to enjoy these special quotes and photographs,
I hope you will be moved to examine and reconsider your own
responsibility as a citizen and guardian of our Earth.

Michael Tollefson
Superintendent, Yosemite National Park

In matters of style,
swim with the current,
in matters of principle,
stand like a rock.

—THOMAS JEFFERSON

The love of wilderness is more than a hunger
for what is always beyond reach; it is also an expression
of loyalty to the earth, the earth which bore us
and sustains us, the only paradise we shall ever know,
the only paradise we ever need,
if only we had the eyes to see.

—EDWARD ABBEY

Mt. Conness from Olmsted Point

Wilderness is a place
where trees grow
that were not planted,
and a man can walk
and he is not
trespassing.

—FRANCES ZAUNMILLER

Alders along the Merced River

In all things of Nature

there is something marvelous.

—ARISTOTLE

El Capitan

Eventually, all things merge into one,
   and a river runs through it.
   The river was cut by the world's great flood and
runs over rocks from the basement of time.
      On some of the rocks are timeless raindrops.
   Under the rocks are the words,
      and some of the words are theirs.
            I am haunted by waters.

—NORMAN MACLEAN

Merced River

Hope is the thing with feathers
That perches in the soul,
And sings the tune without the words,
And never stops at all.

—EMILY DICKINSON

Steller's Jay

Half Dome reflected in the Merced River

One may lack words to express
the impact of beauty
but no one who has felt it remains untouched.
It is renewal, enlargement, intensification.
The parks preserve it permanently
in the inheritance of the American citizens.

—BERNARD DEVOTO

Moonrise from *Gates of the Valley*

There is nothing so American
as our national parks.
The scenery and wildlife are native.
The fundamental idea behind the parks is native.
It is, in brief, that the country belongs to the people,
that it is in process of making
for the enrichment of the lives of all of us.
The parks stand as the outward symbol
of this great human principle.

—FRANKLIN D. ROOSEVELT

Half Dome and the Merced River

Everything has beauty
   but not everyone sees it.

— CONFUCIUS

Snow falling out of oak trees

The Wilderness holds answers

to more questions

than we have yet learned to ask.

—NANCY NEWHALL

El Capitan, Half Dome, and rising moon

Life in us
        is like the water
    in a river.

—HENRY DAVID THOREAU

Redbud and metamorphic rocks

I think the environment should be put
in the category of our national security.
Defense of our resources is just as important
as defense abroad.
Otherwise what is there to defend?

—ROBERT REDFORD

Lake Tenaya

Let us preserve our silent sanctuaries
for in them we perpetuate
the eternal perspectives.

— GREEK PHILOSOPHER

Dogwood blossoms

In the end we will conserve only
what we love;
we will love only
what we understand;
and we will understand only what
we have been taught.

— BABA DIOUM

Great Blue Heron

We have nothing to fear
and a great deal to learn from trees,
that vigorous and pacific tribe which without
stint produces strengthening essences for us,
soothing balms,
and in whose gracious company we spend
so many cool, silent
and intimate hours.

—MARCEL PROUST

Dogwood and giant sequoia

A river seems a magic thing.

A magic, moving, living part

of the very earth itself.

—LAURA GILPIN

The clearest way into the universe
is through a forest wilderness.

—JOHN MUIR

The sequoias belong to the silences
of the millenniums. Many of them have seen
a hundred human generations rise,
give off their little clamors and perish.
They seem indeed to be forms
of immortality
standing here among the transitory
shapes of time.

—EDWIN MARKHAM

Giant sequoias

All those who love Nature she loves in return,
and will richly reward,
not perhaps with the good things,
as they are commonly called,
but with the best things, of this world—
not with money and titles, horses and carriages,
but with bright and happy thoughts,
contentment and peace of mind.

JOHN LUBBOCK

Clouds over El Capitan

Love the animals, love the plants, love everything.
If you love everything,
you will perceive the divine mystery in things.
Once you perceive it, you will begin
to comprehend it better everyday.
And you will come to love the whole world
with an all-embracing love.

—FYODOR DOSTOYEVSKY

Raccoon

Everybody needs beauty as well as bread,
places to play in and pray in,
where Nature may heal and cheer
and give strength to body and soul alike.

—JOHN MUIR

Poppies, goldfields, and baby blue eyes

Spotted owl mother and young

The wild things of this earth are not ours
to do with as we please. They have been given to us in trust,
and we must account for them
to the generations which will come after us
and audit our accounts.

—WILLIAM T. HORNADAY

Mule deer doe and fawn

Man takes root at his feet,
and at best he is no more than a potted plant
in his house or carriage
till he has established communication with the soil
by the loving and magnetic touch
of his soles to it.

—JOHN BURROUGHS

Lodgepole pines, Cathedral Lake

Study nature,
love nature,
stay close to nature.
It will never fail you.

—FRANK LLOYD WRIGHT

Monkeyflowers

When the rest of the primitive is gone,
we still shall have the national parks!

—SOURCE UNKNOWN

Half Dome at sunset

The most beautiful thing
we can experience
is the mysterious.
It is the source
of all true art
and science.

—ALBERT EINSTEIN

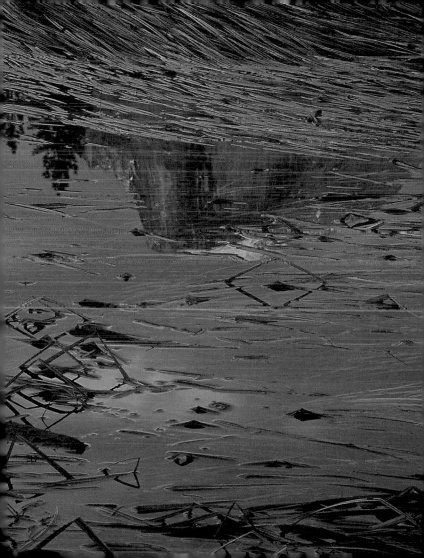

We are the children of the earth
and removed from her
our spirit withers.

—GEORGE MACAULAY TREVELYAN

Pond in Tuolumne Meadows

The care of the Earth
is our most ancient and most worthy,
and after all
our most pleasing responsibility.
To cherish what remains of it
and to foster its renewal
is our only hope.

—WENDELL BERRY

Oak leaves and sunset clouds

There are two ways to live;
        one is as though nothing is a miracle.
The other is as if everything is.

—ALBERT EINSTEIN

Sunset over the Sierra crest

Treat the Earth well.
It was not given to you
by your parents.
It was loaned to you
by your children.

—KENYAN PROVERB

Yosemite Valley from Tunnel View

The nation behaves well if it treats
the natural resources as assets
which it must turn over to the next generation
increased, and not impaired, in value.

—THEODORE ROOSEVELT

Wilderness to the people of America
is a spiritual necessity, an antidote to the high pressure
of modern life, a means of regaining
serenity and equilibrium.

—SIGURD OLSON

Cathedral Rocks reflected in the Merced River

Yosemite Valley, to me,
is always a sunrise, a glitter of green
and golden wonder
in a vast edifice of stone
and space.

—ANSEL ADAMS

Half Dome and elm tree, Cook's Meadow

Water is
the driving force
in nature.
—LEONARDO DA VINCI

Maple leaves, Illilouette Creek

Coyote

Be kind
to everything that lives.

—OMAHA PROVERB

One day's exposure to mountains
is better than a cartload of books.

—JOHN MUIR

The greatest beauty is organic wholeness,
the wholeness of life and things,
the divine beauty of the universe.

—ROBINSON JEFFERS

Aspen grove flooded by beavers

Examine each question in terms of
what is ethically and aesthetically right,
as well as what is economically expedient.
A thing is right when it tends to preserve the
integrity, stability, and beauty of the biotic community.
It is wrong when it tends otherwise.

—ALDO LEOPOLD

Squirreltail barley

The last word
in ignorance
is the man who says
of an animal or plant:
"What good is it?"

—ALDO LEOPOLD

Black bear

Wonder is the beginning
of wisdom.

—GREEK PROVERB

Half Dome and Leonid meteor shower

Both the grand and the intimate aspects
of nature can be revealed
in the expressive photograph.
Both can stir enduring affirmations and discoveries,
and can surely help the
spectator in his search
for identification with the vast world
of natural beauty and the
wonder surrounding him.

—ANSEL ADAMS

PHOTOGRAPHER'S NOTE

Photography can be its own form of meditation—especially in
a place like Yosemite. While exploring the landscape I become
attuned to lines, shapes, and the nuances of light. I have no thoughts
of car payments or book deadlines. For hours I may be aware of
only the plants and rocks around me.

   Others may experience Yosemite through writing, painting, hiking,
climbing, reading, swimming, or just sitting. This national park
protects more than rocks and trees. It is a sanctuary for free thought,
a place where people can contemplate something more fundamental
than asphalt and billboards. What could be more essential?

—MICHAEL FRYE, JUNE 2003

ABOUT THE PHOTOGRAPHER

Michael Frye is a professional photographer specializing in landscapes
and nature. He has written numerous magazine articles on the art and
technique of photography, and is the author of *The Photographer's
Guide to Yosemite*. His photographs have been published in over thirty
countries around the world. Michael lives with his wife Claudia and
son Kevin in Mariposa, California, just outside Yosemite National Park.

YOSEMITE ASSOCIATION

The Yosemite Association is a 501(c)(3) nonprofit membership organization; since 1923, it has initiated and supported a variety of interpretive, educational, research, scientific, and environmental programs in Yosemite National Park, in cooperation with the National Park Service. Revenue generated by its publishing program, park visitor center bookstores, Yosemite Outdoor Adventures, membership dues, and donations enables it to provide services and direct financial support that promote park stewardship and enrich the visitor experience. To learn more about the association's activities and other publications, or for information about membership, please write to the Yosemite Association, P.O. Box 230, El Portal, CA, 95318, call (209) 379-2646, or visit www.yosemite.org.

HEYDAY BOOKS

Heyday Books, founded in 1974, works to deepen people's understanding and appreciation of the cultural, artistic, historic, and natural resources of California and the American West. It operates under a 501(c)(3) nonprofit educational organization (Heyday Institute) and, in addition to publishing books, sponsors a wide range of programs, outreach, and events. For more information about this or about becoming a Friend of Heyday, please visit our website at www.heydaybooks.com.